COACHABLE
BEYOND WINNING TEAMS...
TO CHANGING LIVES

BILL WHITTLE &
DR. DENIS CAUVIER

Cover design by Debraj Dey
Layout by Dr. Jay Polmar
Edited by Debbie Brunettin
Back cover photo by Martin Spicer
Printed in Canada by Gilmore Print Group 10 9 8 7 6 5 4 3 2 1
ISBN 978-1-7777897-5-6

Table of Contents

Note: In full disclosure, Bill Whittle, as a representative of Primerica, earns his income from helping families with their finances and the salesforce he has built. Bill has pledged that he will not earn any money from the sale of this book to any person in Primerica. Bill and Denis have further committed that all of the net proceeds from the sale of this book to any Primerica representative will be donated to charities.

Money-Back Guarantee!

We are so confident in the personal and professional development strategies outlined in this book that we are offering a full money-back guarantee as follows: If, after reading, adopting and applying all of the coaching principles outlined in this book, your life or the lives of the people you are coaching don't change in a positive way, we feel that we and our book have failed you, and we will happily refund your money. And you even get to keep the book. (Please save your receipt.)

Bill Whittle & Dr. Denis Cauvier

Dedication

To my beautiful life partner of 46 years Leslie, my two wonderful children and business partners Blake and Lauren, and their partners Lindsey and Adam, and my two "perfect" grandkids Bentley and Lexie! And to the many coaches for your love, commitment, and dedication in "Coaching" me to be a "better me".

Bill

To my life partner Debbie. She caught my eye in high school and has held my heart ever since. And to the dozens of coaches that have impacted my life beyond measure!

Denis

Foreword

Bill and Denis have teamed up and put together a powerful 64-page guide on how to be successful and happy. The authors make some great points, and one in particular was the dual nature that all successful coaches must first of all be coachable themselves. Two of Coach John Wooden's top assistants told me one of his greatest strengths was that he knew what he did not know.

I have known Bill as his coach and friend for 50 years and have never heard a negative word from him. He lives what he writes in this book and that is, "The biggest reason people resist change is because no one or nothing is that important to them in their lives. The moment that someone or something becomes important enough they will change."

Both of these men live by the philosophy that true leaders teach by example rather than by lecturing others on how they ought to be.

Coach Dale Brown

Hall of Fame LSU basketball coach, motivational speaker and author of several books

Our Accountability Commitment to You

We have taken our combined 70-plus years of experience coaching thousands of people and being coached by some of the brightest people out there and poured it all into this book. Although the book can be seen as a quick read, please don't underestimate the impact that it can have on your life if you are open to it. One of the worst things to do would be to just zip through the pages and do the exercises superficially. Taking your time and being totally honest with yourself will ensure that you get the maximum benefit out of this book. We encourage you to write notes in the book and copy all self-assessments and tools so you can use them multiple times for maximum impact. As Bill often says, "Think in ink" and take time to write good notes.

Our intention with this book is to be your coach and to guide you efficiently and safely from your current situation to your desired future! We are committed to enabling you to bring about a massive impact in your life by helping you achieve your biggest goals and aspirations.

When you are finished reading this book, we would love to hear from you on how it has helped you achieve your goals. Please share with us what specific parts you felt were helpful, what areas you would like to see changed, or what additional areas of assistance you would like in order to help you move on to your next goal. Please see last page of book for email contact.

As you will learn from the book, personal accountability is critical to a coaching relationship–and this is our accountability statement to you, our reader. Please let us know if we have been of service to you!

Best regards,
Bill Whittle & Dr. Denis Cauvier

Introduction

Bill Whittle and Denis Cauvier have known each other for over 20 years. They first met when Bill invited Denis to be a keynote speaker for one of his Primerica leadership conferences. Primerica is a financial services company that operates in America and Canada.

Bill has been in the coaching world his entire life, first as a star basketball player in the state of Indiana, then as a four-year starter at Louisiana State University. At LSU, Bill played for legendary coaches Press Maravich and Dale Brown. He was later chosen to represent the USA at the World Games in Brazil. After playing, Bill began his coaching career at Tara High School in Baton Rouge, LA, pursuing his dream of coaching at the college level. In 1979, he was recruited into the financial service industry where he became one of the top executives with the largest financial services company in North America. He has always been fascinated by the topic of self-improvement, and he teaches that coaching is a foundational leadership skill.

Denis, as a full-time professional speaker, trainer and international bestselling author, travels the world speaking about leadership development and business success. A key component of his message is the power of coaching.

After years of working together doing many conferences, retreats and special training sessions, Bill and Denis decided to collaborate in the writing of this book.

Coaching drives success in companies in many different ways, and there is an abundance of research that proves this point. As you can see from the quick stats below, there is clear proof that coaching, when done well, helps people grow and improve both as individuals and team members.

Coaching Drives Success:

- 22% increase in productivity with training
- 88% increase in productivity with training and coaching combined
- 80% of people coached report increased self-confidence

- 70% of people coached see improved work performance, relationships, and more effective communication skills
- 93% of companies that coach staff report better employee retention
- 92% of business owners agree coaching impact their sales growth and profits.

SOURCE: INTERNATIONAL COACHING FEDERATION

To our way of thinking, coaching is more than creating winning teams—it's also about positively changing lives. We are all on this planet for just a flicker of time, and we have dedicated our lives to helping people move towards their potential. It is with this mindset that we decided to pool our experiences and research to write this workbook-style book. We encourage you to read every page closely and to fill out every exercise carefully, and then apply the tactics and strategies within both as a **coach** and as a **person being coached**.

The term "coach" comes from the old days when people traveled by horse-drawn carriages called coaches. In the West, they were referred to as stagecoaches. Their purpose was to get passengers from one point to another in a safe way. This is exactly what coaches do for people: they help them go from their current situation to their desired place (losing team in sports to winning the championship, or average-performing sales rep to top-selling sales executive) within a safe environment.

Coaching is one of the most important skills for a leader. There are many misconceptions about the top skills required in order to be a successful leader. We have been studying this issue for decades and have summarized our findings in the following chart.

TOP Skills for Leaders

Technical Skills	**O**perational Skills	**P**eople Skills
• Doers • Ability to do things • Based on specific knowledge	• Managers • Ability to organize things • Based on analyzing and planning	• Leaders • Ability to lead and coach people • Based on impact and influence on others

"Leadership at the top of any successful organization is based on:

17% technical skills,

24% operational skills

& 59% People skills."

PART ONE

Being Coachable

*"Great coaches must be able to coach others
as well be coachable themselves."*

~ BILL & DENIS

We called this book *Coachable* because it embodies the two critical elements of every successful coach: they need to *be coachable themselves,* and they need *the required coaching skills* to be able to bring out the potential of their people.

Bill's coaching career started in high school with him playing many sports and continued in college where he was a successful basketball player. He was very open to receiving coaching and improving his game. He studied his various coaches to see what things they did and how he and other players reacted. He coached basketball for a number of years, developing successful teams, before transitioning to the business world where he has coached tens of thousands of people in the areas of financial literacy, personal growth and business success. Despite all of his successes, in sports, coaching and business he is still looking to fine-tune and improve himself. Bill, at 71, has a deep desire to get better and he recently hired Steve Mellor (who has coached medal-winning Olympians) as a coach to ensure that he continues to grow while coaching his teammates to achieve their potential.

Denis's first experiences with coaches were in judo and, years later, in karate. He thrived and won many medals, with the guidance of several great coaches, and he also closely watched various coaching styles. As he was promoted to more senior belts, he was required to coach others. By the time he was 15, most of his students were adults.

Years later, he launched his own coaching, training and speaking business and has coached hundreds of successful entrepreneurs and senior executives including several billionaires. Throughout his career, he sought out many different coaches from different areas of expertise as he pursued his lifelong journey of self-improvement. Denis also greatly values his friendship with Bill and has learned much from him over the years!

*"Coachable people actively seek
learning and personal growth opportunities
that support their biggest goals."*

~ B I L L & D E N I S

The most common challenge faced by the majority of coaches is what can be termed *non-coachable learners.* In this part of the book, we will share why some people are not coachable, signs that someone is not coachable, why people resist change, several self-assessment tools plus much more.

*"The chief responsibility of a leader:
To engage your people by coaching them and turn each
teammate's talent into performance during times of change
and uncertainty."*

~ M A R C U S B U C K I N G H A M

Are You Coachable?

After 70-plus combined years of experience, research, and coaching thousands of people, we have seen a clear and consistent pattern: everyone who ended up being successful had a **coachable mindset**. They were hungry for information; they asked a lot of questions; they sought and applied advice from a host of advisors, mentors, and coaches. They all kept their skepticism and egos in check in order to learn from others and get the edge that they desired so much!

What constantly baffles us is when people ask for coaching but don't take advantage of the advice from their coach. People need to go beyond just *hearing* the message to actually *living* it. If the person seeking coaching is not coachable, the result will be that this person unfortunately will miss out on the wisdom being shared. Being coachable is not limited to plugging into these powerful relationships; it also entails picking up a nonfiction book, and attending seminars and other learning events. It's about constantly investing in personal and professional development.

One of the greatest things a learner can do is to venture further than the role of learner, by becoming a leader and coaching others to help them achieve *their* goals.

> *"Your life doesn't get better by chance;*
> *it gets better by change."*
>
> ~ JIM ROHN

Sharks Are Coachable, Are You?

Kevin O'Leary (right) from **Shark Tank** and **Dragon's Den** TV shows chats with international best-selling author Dr. Denis Cauvier, while filming a segment for the show, which will chronicle his visit to where O'Leary first job was selling ice cream. - **Star Phoenix Newspaper**.

The above newspaper clearly shows Kevin O'Leary highly focused on what Denis was sharing with him. Kevin is not like his television persona "Mr. Wonderful" who claims to know everything about everything—in fact he is very coachable and surrounds himself with advisors. No surprise that he is so successful with his businesses.

Why People Resist Change

The reasons people resist change can best be explained with the acronym "BLOCKED." Anyone experiencing low levels in any of the following seven attributes will find their attempts to change frustrating and unsuccessful–and therefore "BLOCKED." Each letter of the word "BLOCKED" refers to a person's low levels of:

- **B**elief
- **L**ove
- **O**ptimism
- **C**onfidence
- **K**nowledge
- **E**xpectations
- **D**esire

Are You BLOCKED When It Comes to Change? Self-Assessment Tool

Many people are BLOCKED when it comes to change, and so they get frustrated with their lack of success in personal growth and goal attainment. Take the following self-assessment–and be totally honest with your answers.

Instructions: Using a scale of 1 to 5, where "1" means "never applies to me" and "5" means "always applies to me," read the following statements and rate yourself by writing in the number between 1 and 5 that best describes the statement about you. Then, score yourself using the key at the end of the self-assessment.

Statement	Rating
Belief – I don't believe that I need to change.	3
Love – I don't love the goal I am working towards.	2
Optimism – I don't believe that I can change.	3
Confidence – I have doubts and fears that hold me back from changing.	4
Knowledge – I don't know the best path forward to make the change.	2
Expectations – I expect poor or negative results so I say, "Why bother?"	4
Desire – I don't have the willingness and conviction to fully commit to working through the change.	4
Scoring Key: • 7 – 9: Low level of "blockage" to change. • 10 – 19: Moderate level of "blockage" to change. • 20 – 35: High level of "blockage" to change.	22

"The biggest reason people resist change is because no one or nothing is that important to them in their life. The moment that someone or something becomes important enough, they will change."

~BILL WHITTLE

Are You Truly Coachable? Self-Assessment Tool

Most people claim to be coachable, but they're often not as coachable as they believe they are. Take the following self-assessment–and be totally honest with your answers.

Instructions: Using a scale of 1 to 5, where "1" means "never applies to me" and "5" means "always applies to me," read the following statements and rate yourself by writing in the number between 1 and 5 that best describes the statement about you. Then, score yourself using the key at the end of the self-assessment.

Statement	Rating
I can see a gap between where I am now and where I want to be, and I am committed to improving.	3
I am fully responsible for my own life and the decisions I make.	4
I take responsibility for my results even when I am disappointed with them.	5
I am open to exploring ideas and actions other than my own.	3
I am open-minded and willing to receive feedback even when it's constructive criticism.	4
I'm open to coming out of my comfort zone by trying out new ideas, actions, and habits even if I'm not sure they will work.	3
I take action vs just researching or thinking about taking action.	2
I show up for coaching sessions early and am prepared to learn and practice.	3
I do all the assignments, drills, and practice between each coaching session.	3
I realize that major change takes discipline and commitment over time in order for it to happen.	5
I am honest with myself, my teammates, and my coach.	4
I am willing to stop or change any limiting beliefs and behaviors.	3
Total Score	

Scoring Key:
   • 12 – 30: Low level of coachability.
   • 31 – 50: Moderate level of coachability.
   • 51 – 60: High level of coachability.
	42

Once you have answered the above questions, it would be a very valuable exercise to have your coach (the person who coaches you) as well as a few of your teammates (people you coach) assess you with this assessment tool.

Unless you scored high in the level of coachability, you won't be able to fully tap into the power and benefits that a coach will provide. Go back and examine any statement that you didn't rank as a "5" and work on resolving that area of **blockage**.

Pay particular attention to any area for which someone else scores you less than a 5 and resolve to work on this area.

Note: Most people want to change something in their lives but may not be open to change their beliefs, behaviors, and actions. People seek to be comfortable in their thoughts and they fight to protect those thoughts, even when deep down they know that they are limiting beliefs. Larry Winget's book *You're Broke Because You Want to Be* causes most people to get defensive. They say they don't want be poor, and then they offer a variety of reasons why their finances are a mess. The reality is that history will continue to repeat itself: overweight people will remain that way, and poor people will continue to be broke **UNTIL they CHANGE their beliefs, behaviors and actions**! Until they are willing and committed to making some internal changes, they won't get the true value from coaching.

> *"If you keep doing what you always done, you will keep getting what you always got."*
>
> ~HENRY FORD

10 Indicators that Someone is Not Coachable

Review the following 10 statements as they apply to you by marking an "X" in the appropriate spot.

Statement	Yes	No
I talk more than I listen.		X
I make excuses and blame others for my lack of success.		X
I get defensive when receiving criticism.		X
I am not committed to personal growth.		X
I refuse to be held accountable.		X
I am not open to looking at new ways of doing things.		X
I don't seek feedback from others.		X
I feel that I am right and know what I am doing.		X
I settle for average and ordinary results.	X	
I don't actively seek a coach.	X	

Once you have answered the above questions, it would be a very valuable exercise to have your coach (the person who coaches you) as well as a few of your teammates (people you coach) assess you with this assessment tool.

Go back and examine any statement that you or another person has answered with a "No" response and resolve to work on this area.

Apathy and Arrogance Kill Growth

Apathy and arrogance are the two greatest killers of personal growth.

Apathy can be best seen as when there is nothing or no one in your life that is important enough to warrant you making changes to improve.

Arrogance can be best explained when somebody feels that they know everything and that there is nowhere they can improve.

> *"Apathy and arrogance are the greatest dangers to our future."*
>
> ~JANE GOODALL

If you or someone else suffers from either or both of these things, you or they will be truly not coachable—and there is really nothing you can do for yourself or them. Our advice is to be honest with yourself and the other person; be willing to be called out and then call them out on this if necessary. If they still remain blocked with this mindset, go elsewhere and work with someone else who *is* coachable.

> *"92% of people who set growth goals will never actually achieve them because they aren't prepared to personally change."*
>
> ~UNIVERSITY OF SCRANTON

Goals Demands Change

Growth and improvement demand change. The challenge is that most people are very resistant to change. Consider the 40-billion-dollar-a-year diet industry in America where less than 5 percent of dieters successfully manage to achieve their weight loss goal. Sadly, 95 percent don't, and a majority of people actually regain all of their old weight and more. It's alarming to note that, even in severe health cases for which people have needed coronary bypass surgery to save their lives, 90 percent of patients go back to their old behaviors.

These self-destructive behaviors on the surface defy logic. One would naturally ask why would anyone do this to themselves? The real solution to stopping any destructive cycle is to change one's beliefs, attitudes and daily behaviors. Without the needed changes, history will most certainly repeat itself.

It's interesting to note that a goal, in its simplest definition, is a "desired future state." The definition does not refer to the *current* state, but rather the desired *future* state, which implies that some sort of change will need to occur. For example, if your goal is to go to Los Angeles but you're currently in New York City, it will be impossible to get to LA if you don't leave NYC. In baseball, you can't steal second base with your foot firmly planted on first base. So, goals and personal growth demand change—and the bigger the goal, the bigger the change required.

So, the question is why don't most people grow?

1. They don't think they need to change. (Sounds like arrogance.)
2. They don't think they can change. (Learned helplessness vs learned optimism.)
3. They don't know how to change. (They need a game plan.)
4. They don't know who can help them change. (They need to find a coach.)
5. They don't take action now. (Sounds like apathy. Action supersedes everything; intentions mean nothing!)

"It's not what you are that's holding you back;
it's what you think you are not."

~DENIS WAITLEY

The "Case for Change" Exercise

This three page tool captures the reasons a change might need to occur. To reveal the potential reasons for the change, answer the following questions in the space provided in the chart.

Background

- What meaningful goal have I not been able to accomplish?

  Not comitting to starting my buisness.

- How did I get to this situation?

  Procrastination! Self-Doubt!

How Important is it?

- How important is it to me to achieve my goal?

  Very, it will help me overcome other things that make me ~~uncofortable~~ uncomfortable

- What would my life look like and how would it feel to achieve this goal?

  My life will look better finacially and I will feel good helping others.

Current State

- What have I been doing or not doing that has held me back from my goal?

  Being a procrastinator.

Change Needed

- What specific change do I need to make to achieve my goal?

  To be open and start learning

Resistance to Change

What change am I resisting to achieve this goal?

Learning something out of my comfort zone.

Why am I resisting this change?

It makes me uncomfortable

What previous life experiences are contributing to my resisting this change? *Being told "NO", being annoying to people, used to being told what to do, not having the right tools to grow.*

What messages from people in my past are contributing to my resisting this change?

Cold calling people in a previous job when working for a mortgage company.

What is my biggest fear that is contributing to my resisting this change? *Failure.*

What is the worst/best/most likely outcome if I embraced this change? If the worst did happen, how could I cope? Would it really be that bad? *Nothing bad would happen if I embrace this. Missing out on opportunities (worst)*
Best - helping my family and others.

What is my "self-talk" like? Is my self-talk building me up or tearing me down? Is my way of thinking helping me or hindering me?

My self-talk tears me down and is definety hindering me.

What could more positive self-talk be?

Telling myself its ok to be scared but to never fear change.

Which supportive person whom I like, trust and respect, and who has my best interests in mind could help me through this change? (**This is your coach!**)

My sister!

Risks of Not Taking Action

What future problems or missed opportunities are anticipated if I take no action?

I will not make or grow a buisness if I don't start now.

What will be the impact on my life, relationships, career, finances, and how I feel about myself in the future?

I will feel bad for not taking a chance to better myself.

Benefits of Taking Action

What are the benefits if I make the change?

Become financially Stable. Be my own boss. Have more time for me and my loved ones.

What will be the impact on my life, relationships, career, finances, and how I feel about myself in the future?

Final Analysis

Is achieving the goal more important to me than clinging to my past, making excuses, and resisting making the change that is needed?

Yes!

"If at first you don't succeed… try doing what
your coach told you to do the first time."

~ U N K N O W N

What Does Resistance to Change Look Like? Self-Assessment Tool

Most people don't recognize what resistance to change looks like within themselves. Take this quick self-assessment adapted from a recent study by Prosci.com and be totally honest with your answers.

Instructions: Using a scale of 1 to 5 where "1" means "never applies to me" and "5" means "always applies to me," read the following statements and rate yourself by writing in the number between 1 and 5 that best describes the statement about you. Then, score yourself using the key at the end of the self-assessment.

Statement	Rating
Emotion – I often feel fear, loss, sad, angry, anxious, frustrated, depressed.	4
Disengagement – I often feel isolated, ignored, indifferent, apathetic, low morale.	3
Work impact – I often experience reduced productivity, low efficiency, non-compliance, absenteeism, making mistakes.	3
Acting out – I often engage in conflict, arguments, sabotage, overbearing, aggressive, or passive-aggressive behaviors.	1
Negativity – I often engage in rumors/gossip, miscommunication, complaining, focus on problems, celebrating failure.	1
Avoidance – I often ignore the change, revert to old behaviors, avoid responsibilities.	4
Building barriers – I often make excuses, focus on arguing with others, seek out other change resisters, act secretly.	4
Controlling – I often ask lots of counterproductive questions, try to defend the status quo.	2

Again, as mentioned earlier, with all self-assessments, have your coach (the person who coaches you) as well as a few of your teammates (people you coach) assess you with this assessment tool.

Go back and examine any statement that you or another person rate you as a "3 or higher" response and resolve to work on this area.

*"If you don't like change, you are going
to like irrelevance less."*

~TOM FELTENSTEIN

Looking to the Past to Prepare for the Future

Think of a time in your life when you were deeply challenged by a situation and at that time you did not know how you would get through it–but you got through somehow.

Make brief notes below of what happened.

Summarize what happened. *Burst pipe in my home*
How did you feel during the most challenging part? *anxious*
What did you do that helped you get through it? *Called for help.*
What help did you get from others? *They used their Knowledge to fix my problem*
What did you discover about yourself and about others who helped you? *That I can react quickly people are willing to help when in need.*
How might you draw on these resources in the change that is happening now? *I can use them in the future for guidance.*
What specific actions can you take if it happens again? *Call on my support group.*

6 Stages of Change

1. **Awareness** – both self-observance and observance by others.

2. **Acceptance** – not being in denial, a fantasy world, or thinking you know it all.

3. **Affirmation** – the stating of what you want yourself and your business to become.

4. **Action Plan** – a detailed and specific written plan of action.

5. **Action Steps** – this where your daily actions must match your rhetoric.

6. **Accountability** – to yourself and others to stick to the action plan and remain open to feedback.

After reading the above visual, it's important that we don't gloss over these 6 stages of change, as it is critical that you understand and apply them if you truly want to achieve your goals. Over the next few pages, we have explained each stage in more detail.

Ways to Become Aware

The first step of change begins with **self-awareness**. Self-awareness requires maturity, introspection, and honesty to be able to look at oneself and come to the realization that certain things need to change.

Another form of awareness is **other people's awareness**. This happens when you let someone else into your life who can see you objectively and point out an area of change that would help you get to where you want to go.

Jim Kocher, a very successful senior leader in Primerica and close friend of Bill, refers to this type of person as a **Truth Teller**—someone who will share the truth that the other person needs to hear in order to grow, but will do so in a non-confrontational manner with the other person's best interest in mind. A Truth Teller would never put someone down; rather, through their observations and encouragement, they want to push people up, toward their potential.

Funny Mirrors—Distorted Reality

One of the favorite stops at the local carnival is the house of mirrors. The reason it is so popular with people is that, with all the distorted mirrors, there's bound to be one that creates the image that aligns with what you want—i.e., a shorter wider person now looking much taller and thinner. The distorted mirror provides instant gratification when you see what you want to see without you having to put any of the work and changes into it.

A makeup mirror provides a clear and accurate picture of reality in that it shows every blemish, wrinkle or imperfection. Coaches help people see what they **need** to see not what the other person **wants** to see.

Mature people do the opposite—that is, they look in the **mirror** and ask themselves what can they do differently to effect this change. The most successful coaches have developed the ability to hold a mirror up to the person being helped so that they can see themselves in their true light. There is an interesting exercise when looking at body image, particularly for people who deceive themselves and don't acknowledge that they have become overweight and unfit. A great exercise to do is to find a private place where you can remove all of your clothing, place a paper bag with two slits for your eyes over your head and then look into the mirror. This exercise gives you a very clear and honest view of your true body.

*"If you want to see the greatest threat to your financial future
- go home and take a look in the mirror."*
~ JOHNATHAN CLEMENTS

Facing the Facts

The reality is that most people don't want to know what they currently don't know. The great writer Ralph Waldo Emerson said that everybody is seeking criticism but that, in reality, most people are actually seeking praise. Most people say that they want to know, but they really don't. Ask yourself, "Does this apply to me?"

Bill shares that it's interesting to note that over the years, despite the tens of thousands of families he has helped, surprisingly hundreds and hundreds of families have rejected the offer of a free financial needs analysis, which is part of the services that Primerica offers, because they are in denial and don't want to know just how bad their financial situation is. Or the individual who did not want to take a cancer pre-screening test for fear that they might have cancer. Ultimately, both examples highlight the fact that people fear the worst-case situation and feel that there is no solution to either fixing their financial situation or curing their illness.

The real solution is to **face the facts** and get the help needed in order to resolve the issue and move forward—with the help of the right coach. The right coach will lay out a plan to solve the issue, which in turn provides hope and a high likelihood that the future will be brighter than it is today.

Acceptance—Recognizing What You Are Really Looking At

Once someone has removed all elements of self-denial as well as all fantasy and delusions, they can truly be in **acceptance**. This is so much easier to say than it is to actually do—however, once someone can look in the mirror with an objective eye and accept what is there, they will be able to truly embrace the change required to move themselves towards their desired state (goal).

If someone won't fully accept the need for personal growth and change, they won't be very coachable. Consider the "Being Coachable Spectrum" visual below, which demonstrates how people can range from being totally closed (not coachable) to being fully accountable to themselves and their coach (very coachable), and think about how impossible it would be to move towards the right of the chart without self-awareness and self-acceptance regarding the need to change.

Being Coachable Spectrum

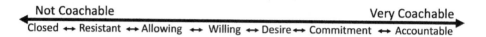

Not Coachable — Very Coachable

Closed ↔ Resistant ↔ Allowing ↔ Willing ↔ Desire ↔ Commitment ↔ Accountable

The Being Coachable Spectrum provides one of the best indicators of where someone is actually sitting, indicating how coachable they truly are. If someone is totally closed to changing themselves, they are 100 percent not coachable. As a person moves along this spectrum, they become more open and committed to changing, until they reach the final stage of being accountable for the change. It is at the fully accountable stage that the person is seen as 100 percent coachable. We see evidence of a person moving through these stages as they increasingly ask for advice and constructive feedback from others, as well as become more open to taking criticism and positively begin to make changes in their life.

To have the most impact, both the coach and the learner have to be at the accountable stage in order for this relationship to really work to its potential.

"Be humble enough to be coachable;
but be confident enough to dominate your position."

~ U N K N O W N

Locking in a Change with Affirmations

Once you have accepted what you need to change, you can lock in this change by affirming the new change. For example, when you have limiting thoughts and beliefs about selling, and you gain an awareness of what these beliefs are and how they are holding back your success, then you come to the acceptance that you need to change your beliefs, behaviors and actions around selling.

You can reframe your beliefs into more positive statements about selling such as: "I like selling. I enjoy selling. Selling is the best way to educate people who need the products or services that I offer." These statements are referred to as "affirmations"–positive phrases or statements used to replace old limiting beliefs.

Positive affirmation statements are a form of self-talk, to program yourself with more confidence in your own abilities. To get affirmations to work, you must see them in your mind and repeat them over and over again. Also, write them down; the process of writing them out helps to further reinforce and lock them into your mind.

5 Guidelines for Making Powerful Affirmations

1. Affirmations start with the words "I am."
2. Affirmations use positive language.
   a. Wrong: "I am not afraid of talking to new prospects." (Use positives)
   b. Right: "I am happy and enthusiastic when talking to new prospects."
3. Affirmations are stated in the present tense as if it is happening now.
4. Affirmations are short, concise statements.
5. Affirmations are specific:
   a. Wrong: "I have a new vehicle."
   b. Right: "I am driving a 2022 Audi R8."

Now, using the above 5 Guidelines for Making Powerful Affirmations, take a few moments to practice writing your own affirmations. You will want to create at least three powerful affirmations for each of your key goals.

Goal: _Become Confident in Myself_

Affirmation 1: _I am ready to make a change_

Affirmation 2: _I am committed to helping people_

Affirmation 3: _I am strong_

"It's the repetition of affirmations that leads to belief, and once that belief becomes a deep conviction, things begin to happen."

~ CLAUDE M. BRISTOL

If You Fail to Plan, You Are Planning to Fail

As Benjamin Franklin said, "If you fail to plan, you are planning to fail." Thus, using daily affirmations to embrace the change needed to move towards your goal is great, but it's not enough. You need to get into positive action, and those actions need to be organized into a logical plan. You will need to figure out the daily actions required in order to achieve your goal, and those actions need to be laid out in your action plan.

Action Means Movement

An action plan without any actual action is worthless. You need to commit to carrying out specific action steps each day that will move you towards your goal. Another way to look at it is your daily actions must match your rhetoric.

Tying Commitments to Results with Accountability

Accountability is defined as *a willingness to accept responsibility or to account for one's actions.* It is the 6th and final stage of change, and it's vital that both the person being coached and their coach are accountable to each other.

"Take accountability... Blame is the water in which many dreams and relationships drown."

~ STEVE MARABOLI

The following accountability tool is designed to identify the top daily disciplines (also referred to as activities) so that both the coach and the person being helped have a clear understanding of and commitment to things that will be done throughout a one-month period.

Fast Track to Success Accountability Tool

This tool is designed to help you and the people you are coaching get on the fast track to achieving your goals. First, it asks you to list your primary goal. With this in mind, you are then prompted to write down why you want to achieve it. To really get the full value of this tool, list the daily disciplines required to move you quickly towards success. Examples of daily disciplines in sales could be: identifying potential prospects; doing follow-up calls; delivering presentations.

My primary goal is ___ to have my own buisness ___

Why do I want to achieve this goal?
To better my life and learn new things

In order to proceed on a fast track to achieving my goal, I commit to the following disciplines/activities this month.

Disciplines	1	2	3	4	5	6	7	8	9	10	11	12	13	14	15	16	17	18	19	20	21	22	23	24	25	26	27	28	29	30	31

Instructions: Introduce this tool to your teammates and have them fill in the chart above. Be prepared to offer ideas of what key daily disciplines will get them on the fast track to achieving their primary goal.

1. In the space provided, write your 10 daily disciplines that will fast-track you to achieving your dream.

   Wrote them on a seperate piece of paper.

2. Each day, after fully completing that discipline, check the box to keep track of your progress.

3. The objective is to fill in all of the boxes during the month. You may elect to be "off" on certain days as long as it doesn't **derail** your progress.

Are you ready to commit yourself to overcoming the temptations of procrastination and to consistently fulfilling your daily disciplines?

Yes _____✓_____ No _____

If yes, sign here: _____

Coach's signature: _____

> *"Accountability separates the wishers in life from the action-takers that care enough about their future to account for their daily actions."*
>
> ~ J O H N D I L E M M E

> *"The worst thing that can happen as a young person, is to refuse to grow up. You refuse to grow up when you believe that someone else must take responsibility for your life."*
>
> ~ S A I D I M D A L A

Sponges, Sieves & Shields

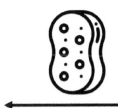 

Accepts All Information   **Assesses** All Information   **Rejects** All Information

There are three types of people when it comes to the receiving of new information. We call them Sponges, Sieves, and Shields and their approach to receiving the information has a huge impact on their ability to be coached and to engage in personal growth.

If you think of a **sponge**, its purpose is to draw in and absorb everything. Little children are like sponges, constantly taking in information that forms how they see the world. The challenge with a sponge is that it can absorb both the good and the bad, and the bad can do harm in the form of limiting beliefs. A sponge is a person that will listen to **everyone** which results in them being pulled in multiple directions and losing their focus.

In many cases, the harm that a young child has experienced causes them to build a defense mechanism, and that mechanism is referred to as the **shield**. The shield is designed to protect them because of the history of what they have absorbed. If you imagine a medieval knight charging into battle, a key part of their armor would be a shield to protect them from arrows, lances, and swords. In this case, having a shield for protection is a good thing; however, some take this too far in that they are extremely closed to new information because they surround themselves with a giant shield. A shield is a person that will listen to **no one** which results in them missing out from the true benefits of coaching.

A **sieve** is someone who is open to collecting all information and can separate the good from the bad. The best filter for a sieve is for them to consider the intention of the source of information. If you have determined that your coach has your best interest at heart, that their intent is pure and they are there to help you grow and achieve your goals, then it is very easy to accept their information, particularly if they have real credibility in that area. A sieve is a person that has the wisdom and discernment to **know who and who not to** listen to.

On a recently broadcasted basketball game, the head coach of the University of North Carolina said that one of his players had stated he was going to seek his own shooting coach. The head coach then commented that if his player was to look up the top three-pointer shooters in college and NBA history, he would see that the head coach was one of the very best shooters, so why was he looking at someone else to coach him when he had one of the best shooters right in front of him? But another way to look at this is if the head coach is so good, why is his player seeking coaching elsewhere? In other words, if the head coach is so good, why isn't the player doing better, given that they are on the same court every day? There is something wrong there.

People who are stuck in the sponge or shield mindset will never truly be coachable. Part of our job as coaches is to help people become sieves—and the best way to do that is to be loving, nurturing and supportive. Remember that King Solomon, despite his wealth and power wished for wisdom above all else.

> *"My best skill was that I was coachable*
> *and aggressive to learn."*
> ~MICHAEL JORDAN

Dependence/Independent/Interdependent Model

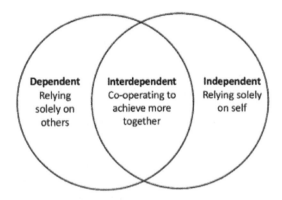

As parents, a lot of people say that the goal is to have **independent** children. When you think about it, people who are independent are removed from and separate from others. If you're telling someone that you want them to be independent, you're really telling them that you do not want to have a close relationship with them.

The opposite of that is to be **dependent** on others. For example, if parents want their children to be dependent upon them, this says that the parents feel weak and need to control their children in order to make themselves feel good. This kind of coach ends up having to call every single play, whether in a game or within business, because the players have never been taught or allowed to think on their own.

Interdependence is when each party does not need the other; however, they want a relationship, and together they are better. Healthy, mature adult children don't need Mom and Dad but want to be with them and appreciate them, and vice versa. The unity that is created with strong interdependent teams is the same and a very powerful component that brings out the very best of the group. It's the perfect example of 1 + 1 + 1 = 10 illustrating the concept of synergy, which is how we achieve more by working together. A great acronym to describe this is T.E.A.M.

Together Everyone Achieves More

"A healthy coaching relationship is one based on two interdependent people committed to helping each other become the best version of themselves."

~ BILL AND DENIS

PART TWO

Being Able to Coach Others

Developing Your People

The most obvious reason for developing your people is to help them to achieve their potential by expanding their beliefs while equipping them to provide the maximum benefit to your organization, themselves, and their loved ones. For team development to occur, you need two key elements: a **leader** who will act as a coach while creating a fun, positive learning environment; and an individual or group who is/are "**coachable**." A coachable person is enthusiastic about developing him/herself, and is prepared to step out of their comfort zone to learn new things.

> *"The number 1 responsibility of a coach is to breathe belief into their players."*
>
> ~VINCE LOMBARDI

After reading the first part of this book, it should be abundantly clear that embracing personal change and growth requires a coachable mindset, regardless of whether you are being coached or coaching others. Having a coachable mindset is critical—but it's also important to know that there are a number of other skills and tactics that coaches need to develop in order to have the most positive impact on the lives of people they are helping.

The **second part** of this book covers a range of topics, including how to confront people, treat people, coach different types of people, develop coaching relationships, develop mental toughness, plus much more.

Care Enough to Confront

Many people say that they want to coach, yet they don't understand that a key part of coaching is to be able and willing to confront with the right intention and skills when something or someone needs to be improved.

Bill shares the story of Bud, a young man he coached who had the potential to become an outstanding basketball player. Bill had tremendous belief in Bud and he wanted him to be not just a great player but a great person. The challenge was that his previous coaches would not confront him on his lack of some basic skills and bad attitude for fear of potentially losing him as a player. The sad reality is that no one cared enough about Bud and his potential to confront him in the area that he desperately needed to develop. Bill cared enough to confront Bud, without being confrontational, the result was that Bud became an all-American and received a full 4-year scholarship.

The key to caring enough to confront is to do so in a kind and compassionate way and not in a confrontational manner. It would be like a man about to leave his home, and there's something not right with his tie, or his shirt is not tucked in properly–his partner should let him know that something is off with his appearance so as to save him the future embarrassment. If his partner were to say, "What is the matter with you? A grown man and you don't know how to dress!" it could quickly become a confrontation–whereas a simple reminder about the shirt would do the trick.

Now reverse the roles, and imagine if every time someone was to confront you your natural reaction was to become confrontational. Very quickly, people will stop investing the time and energy to help you out. It's human nature when faced with confrontation to experience a **fight-or-flight** reaction. If the person opts for the fight, then he escalates the confrontation, and if the person chooses the flight, he remove himself, which may cut off the confrontation but doesn't solve the issue and also does damage to the relationship.

> *"Your job as a leader is to reach through your people's chest and massage their hearts."*
>
> ~ART WILLIAMS, MULTIBILLIONAIRE
> AND FOUNDER OF A.L. WILLIAMS

Late Bloomers

The parable of the Chinese Bamboo Tree explains that, despite planting the seed in fertile soil, four years of nurturing with water and plenty of sunshine, there were still no visible signs of activity or development until, in the fifth year, this "late bloomer" grew 80 feet in just six weeks! Bill shares the story of Monte Rector, a late bloomer who was one of the many young people he coached in basketball. One of the things that Bill always made clear was that the gym would always be open for anyone who wanted to put the extra time and energy into their practice. As a sophomore, Monty, who at that time was small in size and was not all that good of a player, consistently reached out to Bill, seeking opportunities for more coaching and more practice time. The following year, as a junior, he had grown some and had certainly improved his skills. He continued to seek more opportunities for self-improvement, and by the following year, as a senior, he had grown to be bigger, taller, faster—and a much better player. He went on to get a full four-year basketball scholarship. Bill describes Monte as a late bloomer and reminds coaches to have patience with the late bloomers, particularly the ones that are very coachable and eager to learn.

Treat Your People Fair but Not the Same

Successful coaches understand that you treat people fairly but not the same. In fact, if you have three children and you treat them all exactly the same, you're going to mess up two of the kids. In business, as in sports, you cannot treat everyone the same. As a coach, Dale Brown (Hall of Fame LSU basketball coach) understood that different players respond to different things. Where some players respond best to a proverbial kick in the backside, others respond best to a softer, pat-on-the-back approach.

Coach Brown took a group of good players and within one year built a team that defeated great teams with great players. He did this by not treating everyone the same way—whereas the previous coach had placed real emphasis on treating all players exactly the same way. Nick Saban, the great coach in Alabama, takes the same approach, and his results are legendary.

A lot of people fall into the trap of the golden rule being "Treat people the way you want to be treated." The flaw in this thinking is that not all people *want* to be treated the same way. The golden rule in coaching is to treat people the way they **want and need** to be treated, as long as you're being fair with all the other teammates. This approach also applies to recognition and rewards in that *you* might get all fired up to win a trophy or get a T-shirt, whereas the other person might respond better to getting a gift certificate for a meal, a personal development book, or a personal letter or time with their coach.

Make Sure You Treat Your People Fairly

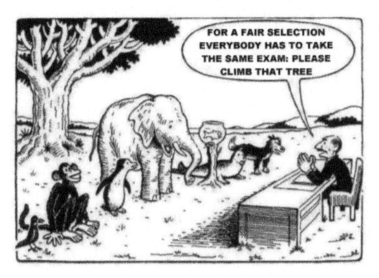

How you treat people is more important than how you train them

Training and developing your people is important for their growth and development—however, **how you treat them** will have an extremely profound impact on how they react to you and to the training they receive.

The keyword in how you treat people is **honor**. When a coach (be it a leader, parent, or employer...) fails to honor people, people fail to honor *them*!

So, the question should be: "How do I honor people?" The four main points to remember about honoring people are:

1. People want to be **Valued**! Honor them as people—not just because they produce results!

2. People want to be **Respected**! Respect different opinions, personality types, views, and beliefs. Remember, if you are the smartest or most talented person in the room, maybe you need a bigger room. Remember, too, that you don't have to be right! It's okay to be wrong. Let your people be okay with being wrong and making mistakes. This is one of the reasons kids (and adults) lie—they are afraid of the ridicule or repercussions of being wrong!

3. People want to be **Trusted!** "Trust must be earned, not given" is a common statement, but it misses the mark as a coaching mindset. Trust must be both earned *and* given—trust from the coach (parent, leaders, teacher, employer...) and trust from the player (child, follower, student, employee...). Remember: **People trust people who are trustworthy!** Ask yourself: "Am I trustworthy? Do I rapidly and freely give trust?"

4. People want to be **Appreciated!** Always remember to <u>criticize in private but to praise in public!</u> Never humiliate, belittle or embarrass anyone! **Be a gold digger!** This means having to dig and dig and dig to find the gold (the goodness and positives in people). If you dig deep and long enough, you will find the GOLD!

The question every coach should constantly ask themselves is: *"How good am I treating my people vs. just how well am I training my people?"*

How you treat people while you're training them, from your tone of voice, your facial expressions, and your body language, needs to reflect how people want to be treated if you want to get the best results from them.

As with the example of the stagecoach, it's not enough just to get someone from point A to point B, but to do so within the most efficient, safe and enjoyable environment.

> *"It's more important how you treat people*
> *than how you train people."*
>
> ~ B I L L   W H I T T L E

Chameleon Coaching

When a chameleon climbs on a tree, it doesn't expect the tree to change its color to match it; the chameleon changes its color to match the tree. The same applies if it leaves the tree and moves to a rock; it will change its color to blend in with the rock. Unfortunately, a lot of coaches expect all of their players to conform and change to be just like them—when in reality they're going to have much more impact if they change their approach to a style that is best suited to support and positively challenge the person they are trying to help to grow.

The Power of Clarifying Intention

A very powerful thought is to consider whether or not the person is worthy of coaching. On the surface, this may sound very judgmental, as if the coach views him/herself as being above other people. Quite frankly that is not the case. A highly dedicated coach will pour much of their life and energy into the person they want to help, and the other person needs to meet them halfway. If the other person's intention is not to get better or to put in the needed work and energy, then quite frankly that person is not worthy of the coach's efforts. Likewise, if you have a learner whose intentions are pure and he's prepared to put in the work and the needed personal changes, but the coach does not have the best intentions, then they are not worthy of being a coach.

Tom Landry (legendary Super Bowl coach with the Dallas Cowboys) would ask each of his players, "What do you want to be: a star, starter, or sub?" He would go further, saying that he didn't care what level the player wanted to play–he just wanted to have clarification on what their intentions were. Once the player shared their intentions, he would say that they needed to understand the price that would have to be paid to deliver at the level that that particular position required. For example, he would often challenge players who said that they wanted to be a star but realistically were not prepared to pay the price of being coachable, being open to change, or putting in the work needed to become a star. He would then wrap up the conversation, agreeing that they hold each other accountable. Mike Haman (lead pastor of the Healing Place Church) says, "When we fail to hold each other accountable, we wind up holding each other back."

Coach Lou Holtz offers three key things that all players want to know:

1. What am I accountable for?

2. Who am I accountable to?

3. How am I doing?

So, as a coach or someone being coached, you need to be able to answer the above three questions. Anyone who is not prepared to be held accountable is not coachable or a good coach.

Motivation vs Manipulation

Manipulation is when you get someone to do something that benefits you and no one else—whereas **motivation** is when you get someone to do something that benefits both you and them. This is an example of a win-win situation. At the very core of the difference between these two words, *motivation* and *manipulation,* are the person's **intention**. For example, when you have a sales leader actively recruiting someone who they think will be excellent on their team, the motivation is to add to the sales team's bench strength and ultimately increase sales and profits for the company—but also to invite the new person to join a winning team in order to experience success and to receive the appropriate compensation and recognition that goes with being a top-performing salesperson. Compare that with the sales leader whose intention is to manipulate his/her people by providing false information and trying to get the team to sell a product or service that is not needed to a potential customer. Obviously, this sales leader has not embraced the true mindset of integrity-based coaching as part of their leadership approach.

Facts Alone Won't Motivate People to Change

It's critical to understand the role our beliefs play in shaping our lives. Our mind automatically reviews our beliefs before accepting or rejecting any new information. It is human nature to **undervalue** evidence that contradicts our beliefs and to **overvalue** evidence that confirms them. We filter out all information that is not aligned with our core beliefs. As a result, we get locked into a circular pattern, a form of "thinking rut," which reinforces our opinions, making it harder to be open to challenge and change these established patterns of thinking.

One of the most common errors made by coaches is to overwhelm the person they are trying to help with facts. If these facts aren't in line with the other person's beliefs, that person may respond by arguing, fighting, or simply walking away. All that the coach achieves with this "fact-dumping" is the reinforcement of the other person's beliefs while eroding the relationship.

Popular social media sites understand this element of human nature and capitalize on it. Various algorithms used by social sites quickly analyze each visitor's position on various hot topics and load people's feeds with posts, articles, blogs, and interviews that reinforce visitors' positions on specific topics. The user is drawn to the social site due to various sources reinforcing their view on that particular topic. This results in the user spending more time on that site and thus being exposed to more information that validates their beliefs. Social media sites understand that a group of like-minded people are worth gold to them because targeted ads are very profitable.

One way to get out of this "thinking rut" is to provide your mind with a way to value your past beliefs while remaining open to new ones. You can do this by acknowledging that your prior belief was the right one given the information that you had at the time. Now, as a growing and maturing adult, you realize, as new information presents itself, that some of your beliefs need to change.

> *"Those who can't change their mind*
> *can't change anything."*
>
> ~ GEORGE BERNARD SHAW

Coaches are Responsible for Creating Team Change

So far in the book we have shared a lot of ideas on how an individual can change— but how can you create a team culture that embraces change? The solution to this lies in the old joke, "How do you eat an elephant?" with the answer being, "One bite at a time." You need to get each and every teammate to change—however, not all people are willing to change.

The visual below shows the **20-50-30 Rule of Team Change**. The rule states that 20 percent of your team is going to be change-friendly, 50 percent will be fence sitters (the wait-and-see folks), and 30 percent will be resisters. So, as a coach, it makes sense to put early change efforts on the 20 percent of your teammates who are more receptive to change. As these people adapt to the change and experience the benefits, this will help the middle 50 percent of fence sitters see the logic of jumping on board with the change. Once 80 percent of the team has embraced the change, this positive peer pressure plus your targeted coaching efforts can help the remaining resisters start to accept, and then eventually embrace it too.

The 20-50-30 Rule of Team Change

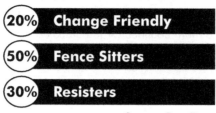

SOURCE: GREG PENN

"Be the change you wish to see in the world."

~ MAHATMA GANDHI

Coaches Need to Understand Stages of Learning

People learn through different stages, and as a coach, it is very important to understand the various stages and how they impact the people you are helping. "The Four Levels of Learning," a great model developed by Abraham Maslow, shows the process of going from unskilled to highly skilled in a specific area. An adaptation of this model is depicted below. Your role as a coach is to guide your people through each of the following phases.

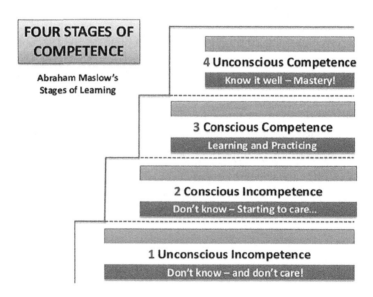

1. The first phase is often referred to as the "ignorance is bliss" phase, in which your learners are **unaware** of their lack of skill. The term *bliss* is used because the state of unawareness is normally blissful compared to being pulled out of your comfort zone. As a coach, you want your teammates to move out of this phase as quickly as possible.

2. The second phase—which we have mentioned before—is the **awareness stage**, which is where your teammates are shown just how unskilled they are. This phase is critical because it will impact their willingness to step beyond their comfort zone. If the process of becoming aware of their incompetence in a particular skill was too embarrassing, they will resist taking on anything challenging. If they are shown in a supportive and non-threatening way that they need to change and develop a specific skill, they will be more likely to embrace change.

3. The third phase is where the **action plan and action steps** kick in. This is where the person improves their skills and becomes very comfortable with the change. One caution regarding this phase is that it can be a dangerous trap if someone remains in it for too long. This is the phase in which people can get locked into a new comfort zone and suffer from the "know-it-all" syndrome. As a coach, you must ensure that neither you nor your charges get stuck here. If the learner stops learning, it is because arrogance or apathy has crept into their mindset.

4. The final phase is ideal from the perspective of **development**. In this phase, learners realize that, despite their obvious knowledge and skills, they still have more to learn. This is supported by positive affirmations such as, "I am a lifelong learner; I enjoy receiving coaching and learning new ways to improve." In this phase, ideally both the learner and the coach are **accountable** to each other. Thus, the learner remains open to continuous learning and coaching even after having attained a considerable degree of mastery.

Training Wheels and Seminars Don't Mix

If you want to teach a child how to ride a bike, you don't sit him or her down in a classroom and give them a long lecture on the history of bicycles or the top 25 points on bicycle safety. First of all, they don't care about all that. Secondly, if it's not fun, they're going to quickly disengage from the learning. The best way to develop a new skill is by *doing* it.

As a parent, you will make sure that they are in a safe place to learn, maybe start with training wheels, and require them to wear a helmet—but the key is to put the child on the bike and let them have fun. The parent, by providing encouragement and praise for how well they are doing, encourages the child to develop even more. The more they are having fun, the more open they will be to ride more. With additional experience comes the development of skills. Soon the child has gone from a tricycle to a mountain bike. This same strategy works with coaching teammates: we must create a fun environment for learning where our people need to be encouraged to "jump on the bike and start pedaling ASAP!"

Analysis Paralysis

One of the biggest stumbling blocks faced by learners who are developing new skills is that of overthinking things. What we mean by this is that some people simply fail to get into action. They get stuck trying to learn and study, overthinking the new skill without actually going out and practicing. Once you have learned the fundamentals, you immediately need to go and practice those skills because real-life experience will ultimately serve you better than an abundance of theoretical concepts. One hour of actual practice will always beat 20 hours in a classroom.

"If you spend too much time thinking about something,
you will never get it done."

~ B R U C E L E E

My Communicating Style Self-Assessment

The following assessment is an adaptation of six of the most popular personality assessment tools in the market.

Instructions: Please review the four words in row 1, going across the page. Ask yourself which of the four words in row 1 is most like you; in the space just to the right of that word, write the number "4." Then review the three remaining words in row 1. Now ask yourself which of the remaining words is most like you. Place the number "3" to the right of that word. Repeat the same instructions, filling in the numbers "2" and "1" to the right of the appropriate words. Now do the same for the rest of the lines in the table.

Please note: you can have only one 4, one 3, one 2, and one 1 in each row. When you are finished, every word must have a number to the right of it.

Dominating		Sensitive		Easy-going		Outspoken	
Inventive		Accurate		Sincere		Outgoing	
Inflexible		Cautious		Indecisive		Erratic	
Confident		Traditional		Likable		Playful	
Productive		Structured		Helpful		Creative	
Controlling		Suspicious		Naïve		Impulsive	
Overbearing		Rigid		Shy		Unorganized	
Guarded		Perfectionist		Stubborn		Exact	
Subtotal A		**Subtotal I**		**Subtotal R**		**Subtotal C**	

Scoring:

Once you have completed the above exercise, please take a moment and add each of the four columns to obtain four subtotals. One final task is to add up the four subtotals; this total number must equal 80. If it does not equal 80, please review your addition.

Interpretation:

Review your four subtotals; the subtotal with the highest number reflects your dominant Communicating Style. Take note of the single letter to the right of each subtotal. That letter corresponds to one of the four styles on the next page. If, for example, your highest column is the first, your Communicating Style is the "A," or Action Style. If your highest subtotals are tied, your Communicating Style is influenced by several styles.

Understanding Communicating Styles

Action Oriented	Analytical Thinker
• Results- and goal-driven • Decides quickly and conclusively • Acts fast in a definite way • Likes to be in charge of situation • Fears loss of control • Impatient and/or insensitive • Dislikes details • Assesses others by their achievements • Inspired by winning	• Logical and controlling • Cautious decision maker • Decisions based on research • Wants facts, details and accuracy • Acts slowly and systematically • Structured, practical and formal • Dislikes impatience, being rushed or disorganization • Tends to procrastinate, be critical, resists delegation
Relationship Builder	**Creative and Expressive Type**
• Very people-oriented • Risk and stress avoider • Cautious decision maker • Dislikes impatience and being rushed • Relationships and communication are important • Wants to be included and accepted by others • Unstructured, creative and relaxed • Dislikes unexpected situations and change	• Creative and entertaining • Decides quickly and spontaneously • High need for socializing and fun • Wants approval and recognition • Seeks freedom to express self • Fast starters, entertainers and effective persuaders • Dislikes details • Resists regulation, routine and perfectionism

Once you have identified your style, ask yourself the following questions:

- What do you think about your results?
- Have you learned anything new about yourself as a coach and how you communicate with others?
- If you look at your lowest style, take a moment to review, as people very high in this style can often be the most challenging for your communicating style to deal with.
- Highly effective coaches are those who can: 1. Quickly identify the communicating style of the person they are coaching; and 2. Naturally shift to the communicating style of the other person. This tactic of meeting others where they are builds rapport, trust, and clarity of messaging. As Stephen Covey said in his book *The 7 Habits of Highly Effective People*, seek to understand before seeking to be understood.

Mental Toughness and Coaching

Successful coaches are both mentally tough themselves and develop mental toughness in their teams. Our decades of research and personal experience have uncovered that being a successful person in all walks of life boils down to being mentally tough and having the right winning attitudes.

As a coach, you need to be mentally tough. We also can't overstate the importance of mental toughness in business. In fact, Denis recently wrote a 96-page best-selling book called *Bullet Proof – Mental Toughness: The Key to Winning in Life*, which focuses on this topic. (Ordering details can be found on the last page of this book.)

Succeeding in business and sports can be tough. The overwhelming majority of successful people would agree that it is not easy. The key difference between people who consistently succeed and those who fall short is the ability to persevere when times are difficult.

Life in sports or in business is an **emotional roller coaster** of ups and downs. People will doubt you and your abilities; you will receive many rejections, face many unforeseen challenges, and encounter numerous negative situations. Product/ service knowledge, selling and customer service skills and a host of other skills will help, but without mental toughness, people will doubt themselves. Eventually, they start to disengage, which is the beginning of the end—unless the person starts to immediately develop his or her own mental toughness. It is critical as a coach that you help your people to learn and to increase their ability to overcome challenges and adversity.

Mental toughness is not about being tough or hard on your people, but it is the ability to *rebound from setbacks and disappointments*, have a strong self-belief, persevere through the challenges, and respond to situations effectively with calmness, focus, and presence of mind. The good news is that you can become mentally tough by developing your inner strength.

The word **STRENGTH** is an acronym developed by Denis to help remind you of the 8 critical components of mental toughness, as shown below:

Stretch beyond comfort zones
Teachable mindset
Resilience during adversity
Emotional maturity
Neutralizing negatives
Goal- and purpose-focused
Tenacity and disciplined and ability to move into action
Happiness, gratitude and enthusiasm

"Failure inspirers winners. And failure defeats losers."

~ROBERT KIYOSAKI

Mental Toughness:
STRENGTH Self-Assessment

The first step towards this is to carry out an honest assessment of yourself using Dr. Denis Cauvier's **8 Dimensions of Mental Toughness Model of Inner Strength**.

Instructions: Review the statements in each of the 8 inner-strength dimensions below and make notes of the areas you are already strong in—and, even more important, identify which areas are in need of improvement as they are holding you back. Don't rush through this exercise; take your time and be totally honest with yourself. As mentioned in all of the other self-assessments, get other people to rate you as well. Identifying areas for improvement and then setting out an immediate plan to improve them will get you on the fast track to success.

Areas of STRENGTH	Yes	No
I fully embrace stretching beyond comfort zones.		
I actively seek the learning of new things, and I have a teachable mindset.		
I keep my cool and stay focused on my goals despite various adversities.		
I control my emotions and reactions to emotional people and challenging issues.		
I neutralize negative news and people by minimizing my exposure to them.		
I am goal- and purposed-focused, and I work daily towards achieving my goals.		
I am disciplined and tenacious, and I don't give up when obstacles and setbacks occur.		
I am someone who is almost always happy, grateful and enthusiastic.		

"You gotta train your mind to be stronger than your emotions or else you will lose every time."

~ DACRAYS

Training and Developing

At the core of all coaching is the training and development of your people. Funk & Wagnalls Dictionary defines these two words as follows:

- **Train**: To improve skills by instruction or practice drill.
- **Develop**: To expand or bring out the potential.

Most organizations focus on "training" their people to "**do**" things better: make more sales; make more money; shoot more 3-pointers—whereas the most progressive organizations "develop" their coaches to develop their teammates to "**be**" better: be a better parent, friend, or player.

We want to be clear that we are **not against training**. In fact, smart coaches understand the tremendous value in increasing a player's skills and knowledge base. What we are saying is that development alongside training is more holistic in nature in that it aims to help your teammates realize their full potential.

Developing your people is to help them achieve their potential while **equipping** them to provide the maximum benefit to the organization. As stated previously, in order for team development to take place, you need two key elements:

1. A coach who will create a positive learning and competitive environment;
2. An individual who is "coachable." A coachable person is someone who is enthusiastic about developing him/herself and is open to learning new things.

Trusting Relationships

Mutual trust is essential for an effective coaching relationship. The more the person you are coaching trusts you and vice versa, the more likely they will be open to your constructive criticism and recommended changes.

So, what is trust? Trust is a combination of two things: **Competency** (the ability to do something), and **Caring** (providing genuine assistance to another person). Competency alone or caring by itself will not create trust.

The model illustrated below shows that if someone is competent but they don't care about me, I will respect them but I won't like or trust them. On the other hand, if I think someone cares about me but I do not feel they are competent or capable, I will respect them but I won't trust them.

Coaching Zones

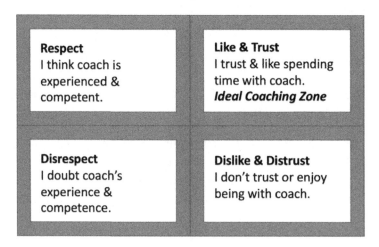

Respect	Like & Trust
I think coach is experienced & competent.	I trust & like spending time with coach. *Ideal Coaching Zone*
Disrespect	Dislike & Distrust
I doubt coach's experience & competence.	I don't trust or enjoy being with coach.

"No one cares how much you know, until they know how much you care!"

~ C A V E T T   R O B E R T

"Player wants to know two things; do you care about me and can I count on you?"

~ L O U   H O L T Z

Coaching Behaviors That Destroy or Build Trust: Self-Assessment

Read through each of the 9 behaviors listed in the chart below and decide for each of the behaviors which side most often describes you. Also have your coach and the people you coach rate which side is most like you. When completed, determine areas that you need to improve in.

Behaviors That Destroy Trust		Behaviors That Build Trust
Not paying attention when others talk	vs	Being a proactive listener
Withholding information	vs	Openly sharing
Acting contrary to your words	vs	Actions that are parallel to your words
Being critical and disapproving	vs	Being accepting and non-judgmental
Acting with a hidden agenda	vs	Being authentic and true to self
Blaming others for mistakes	vs	Freely admitting mistakes and errors
Discouraging others from taking risks	vs	Encouraging others to succeed
Projecting a negative perspective	vs	Having a positive, upbeat outlook
Breaking confidences	vs	Honoring and respecting confidentiality

As mentioned earlier, the goal of the stagecoach is to move from current place to future ideal in an efficient and safe way. However, if any of the four wheels were to fall off, the stagecoach will at best veer off course, or at worst crash.

4 Wheels of Stagecoach (for both parties):

1. Trustworthy and Likeable/Loveable
2. Value provided to other person
3. Committed to excellence and the other person
4. Resolute will to win

If one wheel comes off, the relationship needs to be fixed ASAP!

Integrity Gap

I will do **everything** in my power to actually do what I say I do.
By keeping my commitments it eliminates my integrity gap.
This level of integrity and keeping your word is critical
for both the coach and the person learning!

A Coach's Self-Evaluation Self-Assessment – Adapted from Harvard Business School

The questions below relate to the skills and qualities needed for effective coaching. Use this tool to evaluate your own effectiveness as a coach.

Coaching Skills, Qualities and Mindsets	Yes	No
Are you open to leaving your comfort zone and learning new things?		
Do you provide timely and specific performance feedback to your teammates?		
Do you develop supportive, professional relationships with your teammates?		
Do you take time to observe your teammates' behaviors and attitudes?		
Do you separate objective observations from judgments or assumptions?		
Do you look for signals that your help is needed even if not asked for?		
Do you use pre-planned and in-the-moment coaching sessions as required?		
Do you use open-ended questions to promote sharing of ideas and information?		
Do you use closed questions to help focus the discussion?		
Do you offer recommendations and ideas during coaching discussions?		
Do you confront poor performance or behaviour when required?		
Do you hold people accountable for the commitments they make?		
Do you hold yourself accountable to the people you coach?		
Do you clarify your understanding of the other person's desired goals?		
Do you set a positive tone during coaching sessions?		
Do you demonstrate sincerity in wanting to help your people?		
Do you shift your communications style to better connect with each person?		
Do you focus feedback on the person's behavior and its impact on performance?		
Do you give positive as well as negative feedback?		
Do you always follow up on a coaching discussion to ensure progress?		
If you answered "yes" to most of these questions, you are probably an effective coach. If you answered "no" to some or many of these questions, you may want to consider how you can further develop your coaching skills.		

Once you have answered the above questions, it would be a very valuable exercise to have your coach (the person who coaches you) as well as a few of your teammates (people you coach) assess you with this assessment tool.

Coach's Pre-Meeting Prep Sheet

Meeting Date___/___/___

Meeting Time _____

Meeting Location _____

Teammate's Name _____

Previous Meeting Date ___/___/___

Prepare for coaching session by reviewing the points below.

Explore any follow-ups from previous meeting(s).

Discuss teammate's recent "successes" you have noted.

Explore teammate's SMART (Specific, Measurable, Achievable, Realistic, Time-Oriented) goal(s) they have achieved or are on track to achieve.

Explore teammate's SMART goal(s) that they are no longer on track to achieve.

What specific mindsets, skills or knowledge does my teammate need to develop?

Ask what challenges or obstacles they are facing now. Offer your observations on this.

Seek teammate's suggestions to overcome these challenges or obstacles. Offer your ideas.

Obtain specific actions that teammate commits to and will be held accountable for by the next meeting ___/___/___?

How Well Do I Give Feedback?

This self-assessment will help you measure your current skills at giving feedback. For each statement, check "rarely," "sometimes," or "often" to indicate how consistently you use the described behavior in the workplace.

Statements	Rarely	Sometimes	Often
I pick an appropriate time and place to give feedback.			
I keep my emotions in check, remaining calm and keeping my voice even.			
I provide specific, detailed information about the employee's behavior or performance.			
I explain the impact the employee's actions are having on the team or organization.			
I really listen to the responses of those receiving my feedback.			
I clarify my expectations if there is any confusion about the behavior in question.			
I remember to thank and encourage the receiver of my feedback.			
I provide input as needed in developing an action plan for meeting behavior or performance goals.			
I focus on the steps of the feedback process to keep the dialogue on track.			
I try to understand feedback from the other person's point of view and preferred communication style.			

Of course, *giving* feedback is only half of the story. Take a few moments now and assess your skills as a *recipient* of feedback.

SOURCE: UNIVERSITY OF COLORADO

How Well Do I Receive Feedback?

This self-assessment will help you to measure your current skills in receiving feedback. For each statement, check "rarely," "sometimes," or "often" to indicate how consistently you use the described behavior in the workplace.

Statements	Rarely	Sometimes	Often
I truly listen to what feedback I am receiving.			
I keep feedback and perspective, and I do not overreact.			
I try to learn from all feedback, even if it's poorly given.			
I am willing to learn from questions about my performance or behavior at work.			
I seek feedback, and I attempt to turn every feedback session into a useful encounter.			
I accept redirection and reinforcement rather than denying them.			
I accept responsibility for my role in achieving individual, team, and organizational goals.			
I accept responsibility for keeping my emotions in check during feedback discussions.			
I am committed to listening and learning in all feedback situations.			
I truly listen to what feedback I am receiving.			

How did you score?

How did you score on the two self-assessments? If you answered most of the questions with **often**, your skills for giving useful feedback and receiving feedback effectively are well developed.

If you answered a number of questions with **rarely** or **sometimes**, your feedback skills could probably use more development.

SOURCE: UNIVERSITY OF COLORADO

Talking Through Performance Issues

This tool guides you through a *conversational approach* to resolve performance problems with a person you are coaching. It is based on a simple decision tree model, using a tool that provides a series of 10 questions that elicit yes or no responses. The responses received from the person trigger a specific action or a follow-up question.

Questions (If "Yes" is the response, move on to next question below)	If "No" is the response
Is person aware of their responsibilities?	Tell them what needs to be done.
Is person aware of their performance?	Arrange for performance feedback.
Is person aware of performance standards?	Explain performance standards.
Do they see a need to improve?	Explain the impact their performance has on their and the team's success and obtain commitment for future improvement.
Do they have necessary skills and knowledge to succeed?	Provide needed training and development.
Questions (If "No" is the response, move on to next question below)	**If "Yes" is the Response**
Does the goal appear to be too complex or big for the person?	Consider breaking things down into specific steps towards the overall goal.
Do they lack tools, equipment, materials, funds, support or other resources?	Provide needed resources.
Is their poor performance being rewarded?	Eliminate the inappropriate reinforcers and only reward positive behaviors.
Is their good performance being punished or is there peer pressure against good performance?	Eliminate the source of punishment and reinforce the positive behaviors.
Is the person apathetic, arrogant, negative or unconcerned?	Call them out on this negative mindset.
If you have been through the first 10 steps without satisfaction, the final step is to restate your high-performance expectations and provide the opportunity for the person to improve. If you are still not getting the desired results, then both parties should "face the facts" that this may not be the best fit for a coaching relationship!	

ADAPTED FROM ROBERT F. MAGER & PETER PIPE

Engaged Teammates Stay and Produce

As reported in *HR Magazine,* highly engaged teammates are 3.3 times more likely to be top performers, and 5 times less likely to want to leave the team. The study also found that salespeople who are fully committed to the team outperform disengaged sales people by 82 percent. The same study concluded that 92 percent of engaged people cited **ongoing coaching** as a top priority.

The same principle holds true for all businesses as well as professional sports teams. Superstar top performers have a massive impact on their teams, and this reflects in the compensation they receive. The best of the best who sustain their high performance are highly coachable and are always open for tips, tactics and strategies to gain the advantage on the field and in the marketplace. And they become catalysts to encourage other teammates to adopt the change. Just like we shared in the 20/50/30 Change Rule.

"In order to succeed, the coach needs to pick the right people with the right attitudes doing the right things, and then to put them in the right places at the right time."

~ DENIS

How Well Have You Done in the Past?

Think for a moment about the last few people you have coached, and then answer the following questions honestly:

1. How long has this person been on board?
2. Was the person made to feel welcome?
3. Do you think the person regrets the decision to join your team?
4. Was the person productive and achieving their goals within a short period of time?
5. Was the person recognized and rewarded as they achieved various goals?
6. Did you have a fast-track program to support them, and did you follow it?
7. If you had been in this person's place, would you have been satisfied with the fast-track experience?
8. Did you invest time to develop a positive relationship with this person?

Power of Recognition and Rewards

Look up the words *recognize* or *recognition* in any dictionary, and you will find definitions that use words like "see," "identify," and "acknowledge." These words are at the core of what effective recognition is about. It's coaches caring enough to take the time to **see**, **identify**, and **acknowledge** the organizational contributions, valued behaviors, and good efforts of individual teammates.

Recognition is an essential element to any working relationship. Teammates must know that their work matters and is important to the team. *Nothing propels people towards peak performance like having their efforts noticed, appreciated, and rewarded.* Wise coaches understand and accept that people have shortcomings. However, they choose to focus on their people's strengths while helping their team players overcome weaknesses.

Michael LeBoeuf, author of *The Greatest Management Principle in the World,* said, *"The things that get rewarded get done; the key is to reward the right behaviors."* Some of the most powerful rewards are not monetary. Rather, they are simple, tangible items that propel ordinary people to accomplish extraordinary things. The main point to remember is that it's not so much the reward that counts; it's what the reward represents. We have seen rational adults scramble to win a $10 T-shirt because it was public proof that they'd accomplished a goal for which they wanted recognition.

The best thing to do is to recognize and reward the top 20 percent of your people in a high-energy, entertaining, public forum surrounded by their teammates. There are literally hundreds of ideas for rewards. The key is to have fun and be creative. Remember that not everyone will respond the same to a specific reward—some people don't even want the public attention drawn to them. The key is to fit the reward to what the person will best respond to. Feel free to ask your people for reward suggestions. The following is a small list of possible rewards:

- T-shirts/sweatshirts
- Ball caps
- Plaques/trophies/medals
- Corporate rings/watches/pens/pins
- Certificates of accomplishment
- Gift baskets
- Bottle of fine wine/champagne

- Briefcase/backpack or portfolio with corporate name
- Gift certificate for a restaurant or store
- Trip for two for winning major company contest
- Personal development books/DVDs/online courses
- Winner's dinner with their coach and other winners
- Tickets to music concert or sporting event
- Motivational prints
- iPad
- Public acknowledgement
- Letter of appreciation
- Text/phone calls of encouragement
- Handwritten, heartfelt notes in greeting cards
- Positive talk about someone behind their back so it eventually gets back to them.

"Everyone wears a sign around their neck that says,
'Make me feel special'."

~MARY KAY ASH,
FOUNDER OF MARY KAY COSMETICS

PART THREE

Call to Action

How to Coach Your Teammates on Their Fast Track

The third part of this book looks at how you can help coach your people on a fast track towards their goal. Even if their goal is a major undertaking that will require a long time to achieve, the best way to start is to **start now** and **start strong**.

If their goal is going to take a long time to achieve, make sure that you set things up as a series of growth sprints within a longer marathon. You want to build the person towards achieving each milestone along their growth journey. Remember to offer **praise and recognition** with each growth milestone achieved.

The 11 points below serve as valuable reminders on how to coach your people on their fast track to achieving their goals. After all, the key role of a coach is to help someone get from their current position to future position in an efficient and safe manner.

1. Invest in yourself to become an even better coach by finding a coach who has a proven track record in the area you wish to improve and learn from their example. You need an accountability partner to help you grow and reach your potential. You need to master skills before coaching people.

2. Be coachable *yourself*. Then model being coachable to your teammates, demonstrating how they need to put their egos away and fully tap into a proven system you are sharing.

3. Make sure you and your teammates plug into all relevant training related to your specific goal.

4. Make sure you and your teammates reconnect to each of your "Whys" and primary goals daily. Use the Success Accountability Tool on page 29.

5. Make sure you and your teammates know the top 10 daily dis*ciplines* and do them. No exceptions.

6. Make sure that you and your people don't lose momentum by letting up on the pace of doing the daily disciplines.

7. Help your people and yourself get out of any limiting beliefs. Find things that challenge you and them—and commit to doing them.
8. Make sure you and your teammates focus on "Productivity," not just "Activity" that moves each of you towards your goals. Don't just be busy spinning your wheels—instead, get productive with actions that create real results.
9. Hold yourself and your teammates accountable for commitments to each other.
10. Create a friendly, competitive atmosphere while keeping score of your and all of your teammates' performances. An example is a quarterly sales contest where everyone competes in a fun and supportive environment that nurtures growth for each teammate.
11. Make sure to recognize key improvements and performance milestones. Examples of key milestones in a sales contest could be reaching predetermined sales targets and growth over the previous three months.

> *"Today I will do what others won't so*
> *tomorrow I will do what others can't."*
>
> ~ J E R R Y   R I C E

We hope that you have enjoyed the material and have found it and the self-assessments in this book to be useful as you and your teammates move towards achieving your goals. You now know that being a coach is so much more than a title or a label on a shirt. *It's a mindset of mutual commitment and accountability rooted in service and the well-being of others that goes beyond words into real actions.*

As we mentioned at the beginning of this book, a coach is someone who takes you from your current place to a future place. The real measure of a successful coach is someone who can both reduce doubts and fears and increase confidence and beliefs in their people. Please remember that true coaching goes beyond winning teams and is ultimately measured in the lives you change. **The true legacy of the best coaches is that not only do they change the lives of those they train, but the people trained go on to positively impact so many others.**

Bill has shared the following powerful story on hundreds of stages:

The terrorist attacks of 9/11 on the United States were a massive shock that was felt around the world. Reports soon emerged after the unprecedented tragic events of various everyday people, from first responders to ordinary citizens, who stood up and helped the people around them. One particular incident is United Flight #93 that was scheduled to fly from Newark to San Francisco. After 46 minutes, terrorists took control of the plane and announced to the passengers: "There is a bomb on board. Sit down!"

One of the passengers was 32-year-old Todd Beamer, a married man and father of three young children. Beamer and other passengers quickly realized that the intention of the terrorists was to crash into either the White House or the U.S. Capitol Building. Beamer, while attempting to contact his family, was connected to Lisa Jefferson, a GTE airphone supervisor. They spoke for thirteen minutes, and recited the Lord's Prayer and Psalm 23, with other passengers joining in. After a few minutes, the plane started to dive. Todd remained calm. "I'm still here," Lisa said. "I'll be here as long as you are!"

At that point, Beamer and a group of passengers and flight attendants huddled together and voted to storm the cockpit. The last words heard from Beamer were: **"You ready? Okay, let's roll!"**

There were no survivors on that plane, but because of the courageous decision made by Beamer and the others, thousands of lives were saved!

After reading *COACHABLE: Beyond Winning Teams... To Changing Lives*, Bill and Denis ask and challenge you:

"YOU READY? OKAY, LET'S ROLL!"

Bill and Denis are open to partnering with select charities to use this book as a fundraiser. If you would like to explore this possibility please email: denis@deniscauvier.com

To inquire about bulk book order discounts or having Dr. Denis Cauvier or Bill Whittle speak at your next event:

Email: denis@deniscauvier.com
Text 1.613.864.7750

If you enjoyed this book, you might enjoy *Bullet Proof Mental Toughness the Key to Winning in Life* by Dr. Denis Cauvier

To order additional copies of **Coachable: Beyond Winning to Changing Lives** or **Bullet Proof: Mental Toughness, The Key to Winning in Life** go to:

American orders please visit: DigitalPFS.com

Canadian orders please email: denis@deniscauvier.com